QUIET BEAUTY OF **CHINA**

by Pat Fok

RIZZOLI
NEW YORK

Editor: Mavis Guinard, Buchillon (Switzerland)
Art director: Julien van der Wal, Geneva (Switzerland)

First published in the United States of America in 1987 by
RIZZOLI INTERNATIONAL PUBLICATIONS, INC.
597 Fifth Avenue, New York, NY 10017

ISBN 0-8478-0859-9
LC 87-45447

Printed in Switzerland by IRL Imprimeries Réunies Lausanne s.a.

TABLE OF CONTENTS

TO ALEXANDER LINGSHAN

INTRODUCTION

"Quiet Beauty" seems an unlikely title for a book on China—a country of over one billion people. I think, though, that quietness is an attitude, an ability to stand with total inner peace even in a crowd. Beauty is not just the ethereal mist that enshrouds Huangshan or the unusual rock formations of Guilin. Beauty can be found in an old man doing his leg exercises in the compound of the Temple of Heaven, or in people pushing their bicycles uphill in the shadow of the Great Wall silhouetted against a hazy winter sky. I choose not to include in this book the highrises of Beijing, the super highways of Guangzhou, the industrial buildings of Shanghai. I select intimate corners of China that may someday give way to modernization. Gone already are many little wooden houses and cottages curtained by bamboos to make way for progress. I was told that a cable car now whisks tourists up and down Huangshan, the Yellow Mountain. It took me days, just like the Tang Dynasty poet Li Bo, to walk up the mountain. I prefer it that way. In anticipation, one creates a dream. Our vision is colored by our imagination.

I like the freedom of traveling alone, being able to decide from one moment to the next where to go, when to pause. Following my own pace in walking, climbing, I have an intense dialogue with nature, guided by my own instincts to the vantage point, to the right moment to enjoy China's quiet beauty. In silence, I focus on the unusual, the amusing, the beautiful, releasing the shutter at the split second it exists. I read few guide books before setting out. I do not want to spoil my first impression with preconceived ideas and secondhand notions. My trips took months of planning; my sojourn in each place never more than a few days. Some routes were arduous. The approach to Huangshan took over two days in the fog, scaling precarious steps, thousands of them.

Quiet Beauty is born in the mind. Li Bo in his drunkenness may have seen beauty effortlessly; my more sober mind requires energy to find and recreate some of what he described in his verses. I must choose where to point my camera.

That certain quiet beauty can best be appreciated if one ventures ahead of others. I was in Guilin over ten years ago. Nearby Yangshuo, long the most celebrated scenic spot in China, did not yet have electricity: it had been closed to outsiders for over twenty five years. I was able to retrace some of the early experiences of another poet, Han Yu, sailing down the River Li in a small boat and waking up to the sound of oars. Today, Guilin is very much discovered and on the itinerary of many tours to China, only a direct easy flight from Hong Kong. I prefer not to return. I know my first experience to be more akin to what originally inspired me to go there.

> The river like a blue silk sash
> The hills like hair pins of jasper jade

wrote Han Yu of Guilin and the Lijiang river in the eighth century. Guilin is true to the romantic image of a traditional Chinese landscape—miniature hills with unusual profiles reflected in the clear water. On the hills are pagodas, and little boats sail down the gentle river. To the observer, everything is to scale, creating a feeling of intimacy and coziness. I found Guilin poetic. By contrast, Jiuzhaigou indeed presents an untamed, wild beauty. The lakes are a vivid turquoise, and the hills ablaze in orange and yellow, a symphony of colour in autumn. A hundred lakes spill over into giant waterfalls. The Falls of Nuorilong are a hundred meters wide, thundering and powerful.

I ventured into Tibet and photographed the Potala palace which rises majestically on the Red Hill in Lhasa. It is the highest palace in a land known as the roof of the world. Golden in the sunlight, it was by moonlight that I most enjoyed the Potala. I had no tripod with me, relying on a rock as a support on which to lean my camera and using my cable release to record this vision.

There were trips that did not come up to my expectations. My information was totally out of date when I took the journey down the Yangzi River, guided only by my imagination and Li Bo's poems describing the trip as both spectacular and dangerous:

Struggling Up the Three Gorges

The Wu Mountains squeeze the slender blue sky
Making the Pa River rush down through the tortuous Yangzi Gorges.
The Pa waters might pass and turn suddenly away,
But the slender blue sky would remain there forever.

For three mornings my boat struggled by the Yellow Cow Peak
And another three evenings too slowly had I been proceeding,
Gazing still at that high peak for three weary mornings and evenings.
Unwittingly my hair turned to white threads.

And going downstream:

Leaving White King City

Early at dawn, I left White King City high amid colored clouds,
What a voyage—to reach Jiang Ling in one day, a thousand li away!
While the little monkeys kept up their unceasing chattering on both cliffs,
My light boat had already slipped past ten thousand mountains!

I realized later that his descriptions of the journey down the Yangzi were fitting only before the river was tamed by modern day technology. I took my son, then aged six. We were both ready to face the perils of the trip, only to experience a calm cruise, traveling most of the time in fog while a loudspeaker announced occasionally what we were missing. In the three days that we sailed down the Yangzi, I only took out my camera twice. On another trip, I came to Suzhou, south of the Yangzi. Marco Polo called it the "Venice of the East." The little canal houses rising straight out of the water transported me back in time.

There is so much scenic treasure in China that especially in the earlier years of my travels, I often came upon the unexpected. On my way to Mount Emei, we made a stop at Leshan in Sichuan. I wasn't prepared to see such a grandiose statue of Buddha, seventy-one meters tall—almost eighteen meters taller than the Stone Buddha in Bamian, Afghanistan that is claimed to be the "tallest stone Buddha in the world." Begun in the year 713, it overlooks the confluence of the Qing Yi, Dadu and Minjiang Rivers.

I first photographed China in 1973, after its long years of isolation, in a manner best described by Christopher Isherwood: "I am a camera with its shutter open, quite passive, recording, not thinking..." Today, I am more actively seeking, guided by the spirit of ancient poets, painters and travel writers. A line of classical poetry, a photograph spotted in a magazine, a friend who tells me of a hidden and beautiful place, hearsay, a fairy tale, a painting will set my imagination going and my bags are packed.

HUANGSHAN
THE
YELLOW
MOUNTAIN

HUANGSHAN

Sometimes, in my travels, I encounter places to which I feel an immediate rapport, a presence of what the Chinese call "Ling Qi", a magical spirit of enchantment. When I visited Huangshan, I strongly felt that I was in an epicenter of "Ling Qi", in a place inhabited by gods and spirits, as Mount Olympus must have been to the ancient Greeks.

Huangshan, until a few hundred years ago, was remote. Poets, painters and scholars who ventured there reached only a few of its peaks: the White Geese Mountains, the Cinnabar Well, the Lotus Flower Peak and the Prime Minister Spring. After the fall of the native Chinese Ming Dynasty to the invading Manchus in 1644, many scholars withdrew from their government positions to become monks. The best known painter of the period, Hong Ren, spent most of his remaining years as a monk in the vicinity of Huangshan. He developed what is known as the "Anhui School" of painting, typified by landscapes with no people, reflecting a yearning for the purity and constancy of nature far from the confusion of the human world. They painted in the abstract manner, dry and linear in style.

The popularity of Huangshan grew as new access became available. Subsequently, temples and villas for wealthy merchants were built. Huangshan, with its twisted pines, sharpcut rocks and clouds, is often in the paintings of Mei Qing and Shi Tao in the third quarter of the seventeenth century. They painted the Lotus Flower Peak looming out of the mist, the One Hundred Cloud Ladder winding up the rocks to the sky and travellers bathing in the Hot Springs Pond. In contrast to Hong Ren and his contemporaries, these artists de-emphasized the hard-edged contours and concentrated on the peculiar, sometimes anthropomorphic rocks as well as the misty expanses between the peaks.

Legends and stories sprang up about the origin of Huangshan. One ancient tale attributed its creation to a painter.

"In very ancient times lived a great painter, Pei Du. Even as a child, by the age of ten he had learned all he could from all the great masters of China. He set out to paint all over the country. Now, in those days, China was flat. But Pei Du painted mythical mountains, sharp rocks and cliffs, pines, mists swirling, a bird here and there, sometimes a solitary person or a lone mountain bridge or hut, a wistful wilderness. Those things he had only seen in his imagination and in his dreams. He sought perfection in each stroke of his brush as he continued day by day and year after year to paint over and over each element of his landscapes. Many people flocked to catch a glimpse of his paintings just before he had finished them because as soon as they were completed, he would destroy them the next morning as too imperfect to be preserved. Pei Du continued to paint until he was an old man. When he was ninety years old, his work had come to the attention of the god of beauty, Huangshu, who one night appeared in a dream. The god told him that he would have time to paint only one more picture before his death, and it was to be perfect. Pei Du spent the next ten years working on that single painting every day. It was finally finished the day before his hundredth birthday. On that night, the god of beauty, again appeared in his dream: 'You have succeeded, Pei Du. Tomorrow, you shall paint with us in heaven.' The next morning before dawn, Pei Du rose and sat quietly in front of his painting. Thousands of people had already gathered, waiting for the night to pass to see the finished picture. But the mists had risen in the night so no one could see anything. When it finally began to clear, the gigantic painting appeared, part by part. Everyone gasped. Many cried. Sheer beauty overwhelmed the souls of all present. There was no doubt that the painting was perfect. Pei Du's eyes misted with tears. It was the most beautiful work of art that ever was or would be created. As dusk came, Huangshu, appearing in the form of a white mist, dissolved the painting into reality. Seventy-two peaks emerged, with streams, forests, waterfalls, hot springs, trails and bridges. A temple stood in the foreground, a lotus-like summit on one peak. When the people had recovered from their shock, they looked at Pei Du. His eyes were closed. There was a smile on his face. He was dead. But his painting was perfect, and it is now a place called Huangshan, an enchanted mountain."

There is no historical record of Pei Du, but I like to think of the extraordinary shapes of Huangshan as born by magical rather than by geological causes.

I came to Huangshan via Hangzhou, two hundred and eighty-three kilometers away, having spent eight hours on a dust road. In the month of May, the setting was harmonious, a wonderful prelude to my pilgrimage up the mountain. I stopped overnight in the Tao Hua Hotel, a simple guest house at the foot of the mountain. The next morning, I chose the eastern, more scenic ascent in preference to the more popular western route which, though longer, is not as steep. The handhewn steps seemed to lead to the sky, never ending, so narrow that only one person could pass at a time. I spent the whole day walking in the fog, seeing none of Huangshan's famed scenery, but trusting that the god of beauty would unveil it for me. I spent that night on Yuping Feng (Jade Screen Peak) in a halfway house, once a temple.

Photographing Huangshan presented a great challenge: not only physically demanding with tens of thousands of steps to scale, but with the added uncertainty whether, after the climb, one could see any of the beauty preconceived in the mind from the writings of Li Bo, Wang Wei and the paintings of Hong Ren. The seas of clouds occur after the rain and last but a fleeting moment. The mists curl and shift continuously. The photographer's challenge is also a photographer's dream because of the opportunity to capture unique moments. No two pictures of Huangshan look alike. That May, I was fortunate to enjoy good weather. I took most of the photographs just after a downpour followed by a spell of hazy sunshine. In bright sunlight, the peaks of Huangshan look stark and harsh, the rocks sharp and deeply fissured. Aside from the twisted pines, there is little vegetation to soften the severe outline of the cliffs. The combined effect of mist and softer light is essential to bring out the beauty. Li Bo wrote of Huangshan:

> Huangshan, four thousand feet above the earth,
> Two and thirty lotus peaks,
> Stone pillars, crimson cliffs,
> Golden buds and open blooms.

I used to climb the mountain's highest summits,
And there gaze upon the pines of Mount Tianmu.
There, the immortal once refined elixir,
He took wing, and left but footprints...

My experience of Huangshan was no less moving; when the fog cleared, I watched the scenery of Huangshan change from sunrise to sunset. In sun, mist, rain and snow, the mountain showed a myriad faces. For thousands of years, poets, artists and travellers came to Huangshan for its clouds, pines, and rocks. Lotus Bud Peak, Scissors Peak, Greenery on Writer's Brush Point Peak stand among the seventy-two peaks etched against the sky among the clouds, unique and awesome. High on the cliffs are four rocky pillars in human form: in the center, they are "Two Immortals Playing Chess," on the right, "The Prime Minister Watching a Game of Chess," on the left, "The Immortal Making Sacrifice." Their striking shapes have inspired many painters. Some rocks are big, some small, some recline, some resemble a man or an animal and others just rise like capricious stalagmites. One boulder, called "The Rock that Flew from Afar," looks as though it had been carelessly dropped on the top of the mountain. At the summit of many peaks barely two or three people can stand at one time.

Higher up on Huangshan, the pines have withstood frost and snow for generations. They grow in strange and fascinating ways, some intertwined, some solitary. Often one rises from the sheer cliff in a most unlikely place. Their roots are unusually long, many times the length of the trunk, extending deep into crevices where there is no apparent soil on the bare crag. Almost all lean to the south with no branches on the cold windswept side exposed to the north. The winds fan out the branches and needles, bend the trunks into whimsical shapes. They also bear whimsical names. I found the "Welcoming Pine" and the "Pine Saying Farewell" that I had read about in poems.

When I reached the Lotus Flower Peak (at eighteen hundred meters, or almost six thousand feet), intermittent sunshine and rain formed Huangshan's dreamlike rising mists draped around the jagged peaks, just as one sees in some of the Chinese land-scape paintings. Every moment, clouds and mist shifted.

One morning, before five a.m., I was crouching on the very top of one peak waiting for daybreak. Gradually, the sun illuminated the silhouettes of the other peaks and the odd-shaped rocks. A "Lotus Flower," a "Fairy's Boot", a "Monkey Contemplating an Ocean of Clouds" came into view. The quiet was eery, though I was not alone: ten or twenty dark figures also crouched on various vantage points to watch nature's magic. Suddenly, I heard "Tai yang chu lai le." ("The sun is out"): that was our great reward for sitting in the cold, having walked and climbed from everywhere. Still it was a very private moment—my own dialogue with the mountain around me.

The scenery is at its most poetic when you have the good fortune to see it, as I did, after rain showers with clouds billowing up among the peaks. I raced from one summit to the next, trying to photograph each transient moment. I was unable to rest in my comfortable room at the guest house knowing this ever changing beauty was outside.

During the Ming Dynasty, a travel writer, Xu Xiake, had heard of the exquisite beauty of Huangshan. He went there, time and again. It was as though the gods were trying his patience. He saw none of the famed beauty: the mountains were always shrouded in fog. When, finally, after yet another trying ascent, he saw Huangshan suddenly in its full splendor with the peaks, rocks and pines emerging from the mists and clouds, he exclaimed: "Now I believe that such beauty indeed exists." Hence, the peak he was admiring just then is still known as the "Now I Begin to Believe Peak." He wrote: "Once you have visited Huangshan, it is not necessary to see the others," referring to the five great mountain ranges of China: "It has the magnificence of Taishan, the sharpness of Huashan, the mists and clouds of Hengshan, the cataracts of Mount Emei."

For me too, since my visit to Huangshan, no other mountain has ever seemed as beautiful, no other mountain as grand.

應是天公醉時筆　重重粉墨尚縱橫

萬木雲深隱

碧落留雲住

只疑片片雲連海　不信茫茫海是雲

待欲乘風杭一葦　三山上謁玉虛君

是畫不知還是夢

空山新雨後

JIUZHAIGOU
AND
THE YELLOW
DRAGON

九寨溝

JIUZHAIGOU AND HUANG LONG, THE YELLOW DRAGON

Discovered accidentally by loggers, Jiuzhaigou—a remote area in the province of Sichuan, is one of the most extraordinary parts of China. In autumn, its foliage and its mirror-like lakes spilling into waterfalls are uniquely Chinese. I traveled with my son Lingshan (then six years old) by Land Rover. Because the road from Chengdu, capital of Sichuan, to Jiuzhaigou was unpaved, the four hundred and seventy kilometer journey took over two days. Part of the way, we drove beside a sheer drop of several thousand feet, our road a narrow band between the mountain and the turquoise lake far below. The driver carefully avoided occasional fallen rocks. He told us a city had slid into this lake in 1960 during an earthquake. This bit of information heightened the drama of the jagged landscape. After a twelve hour drive, we stopped for the night in Songpan, two thousand eight hundred meters above sea level. The town was covered with snow and the temperature had dropped thirty degrees from that of Chengdu when we had set out at nine o'clock that morning.

The second day, we continued our journey along the River Min (Minjiang), a tributary of the Yangzi, to climb up to an altitude of three thousand one hundred meters. It was like the Swiss Alps in winter, except for the tribal dwellings. There were clusters of a dozen wooden houses with slanted roofs and colorful banners waving in the air. Tibetan herders walked in the snow beside their long-haired cows.

We sidetracked off the main road to Jiuzhaigou to visit the Huang Long or "Yellow Dragon", where three thousand four hundred terraced, shallow pools reflect the surrounding peaks. The three and a half kilometer "Golden Sand Paved Road" looks indeed like a golden dragon flying up the snowy mountain. And, from a distance, the bumps of the slope with water coursing over them do give one the impression of a dragon's gigantic scales. We waded ankle to knee-deep against the rushing water for two hours up to the peak, passing cascades and curtains of falling water. It is a mountain of legends, an enchanted place... At the summit, I had a spectacular view of the Yellow

Temple built in the Ming Dynasty by Tibetan Buddhists: fresh snow frosted the brown roof, pools of emerald and aquamarine sparkled in the distance. Close up, prayer scrolls in Tibetan dangled from a yellow conifer. The temple seemed deserted. Its walls were covered with ancient poetry.

We continued our journey on a very uneven road to arrive in Jiuzhaigou three and a half hours later in the dark. China's Premier, Zhao Ziyang, came here in October 1983. He exclaimed: "Guilin is most beautiful, yet Jiuzhaigou surpasses Guilin." I was aware of plans to build a helipad to make this hidden, almost virgin forest with its hundred lakes and giant waterfalls more accessible to tourists. I wanted to see it in its untouched beauty. Thus, in October 1984, I found myself in Jiuzhaigou.

Nine Tibetan tribes had lived in this region before it was "discovered." An elderly man of Tibetan ancestry traced its origin back to a legend: "Once upon a time, in the wooded hills of Jiuzhaigou lived a god named Dage and a beautiful goddess named Wonuosemo who fell in love. To show his love, he presented her with a gift, an elegant mirror elaborately wrought from wind and clouds. By accident, she let it slip from her hand: the mirror shattered into many pieces which turned into the one hundred and eight lakes."

Jiuzhaigou—"Nine-Stockade Gully"—is formed by three major gullies, at two thousand five hundred meters above sea level. The name came from the fortified, "stockaded" hamlets where Tibetan minority settlers lived in the past. Today, it is two hours by plane from Tibet. How the Tibetans originally arrived there is a mystery. Some very rare trees and plants remain from primeval times and, in addition to pandas, other splendid animals such as the golden haired monkey and the river deer can still be found here.

Few places live up to one's expectations. Jiuzhaigou is an unusually fulfilling experience. The "Five Flower Lake" with its crystal clear waters reflecting a medley of colour, red, green, deep blue, yellow, was an abstract painting. I saw a white horse standing in the azure water of the "Arrow and Bamboo Lake", nibbling at branches overhead. Not far away, a cone shaped hill jutted from the ground: the "Sword Cliff" dressed in its autumn colours. The most famous falls in Jiuzhaigou are the Nuorilong

Falls where the three gullies meet: one hundred meters of tumbling waters. I climbed halfway up a hill facing the falls until I could see their very top: what a surprise to see a small wooden house by the lake with another torrential waterfall beyond it. Later, we drove past a reed pond and came upon a tranquil widening in the clear stream.

This was a world one could only appreciate by respecting its silence enhanced by the roar of the waters. In Jiuzhaigou, I found my dream down a forgotten path that led to three wooden sheds with waterwheels. Two were still grinding away, grinding corn for the Tibetans. I walked into the abandoned mill, no larger than a hundred square feet. Through a small opening in the wall, I saw a Tibetan girl washing clothes in the river. Another headed uphill, buckets of water balanced on a bamboo pole. That was October 20, 1984. A distant past, a world away.

夜宿峯頂寺　舉手捫星辰

44

不敢高聲語　恐驚天上人

清溪清我心

桃花流水窅然去　別有天地非人間

疑是銀河落九天

湖水林風相與清

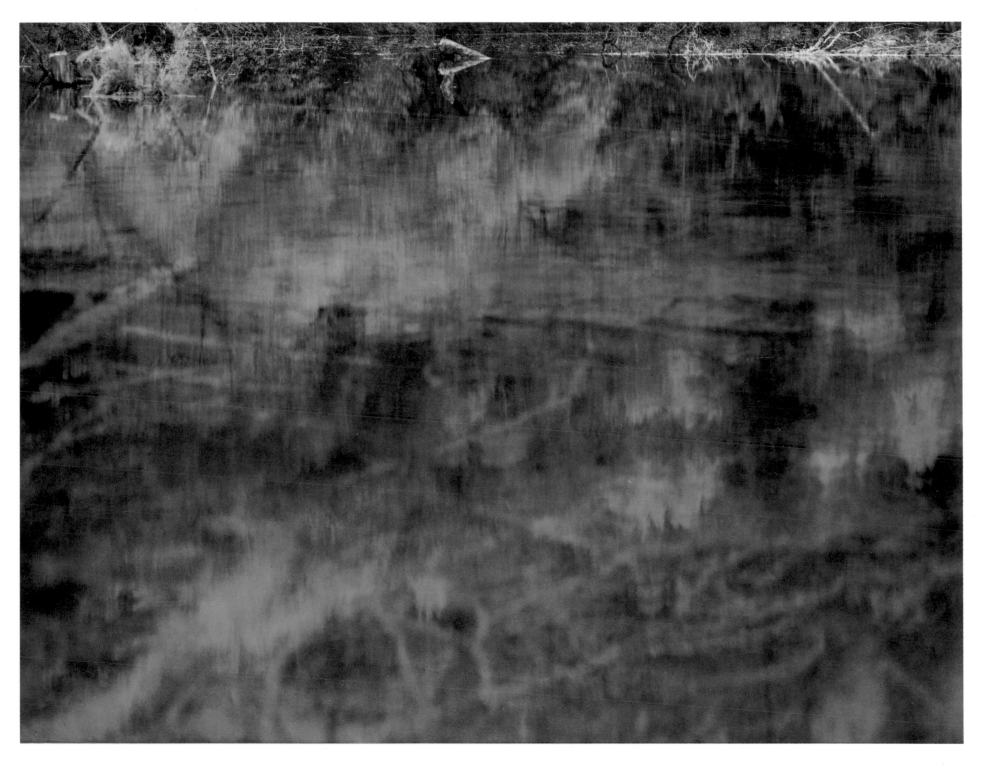

秋水清無底

GUILIN

GUILIN

In the south of China the capital of Guangxi province, Guilin, "Forest of Osmanthus," is named after a tree with fragrant white flowers. There are more than a hundred thousand osmanthus trees in the town. Flanked by the Li and Tao Hua rivers, long celebrated as the most beautiful place in China, "Guilin's mountains and rivers reign supreme in the world." A poem by Han Yu compares the River Li to a blue sash and the surrounding hills to jasper jade hairpins. I was awed by the Matterhorn in Switzerland where mountains are renowned for their size and majesty. I spent a summer photographing mountains in California's Yosemite National Park with America's nature photographer, Ansel Adams. But, not until I was among the miniature mountains of Guilin, reflected in the River Li, did I feel part of the natural beauty that surrounded me. Unlike the other mountains where I felt dwarfed, the hills of Guilin seemed to be in scale with the observer. In the West, a mountain is a challenge. A Chinese mountain typified by those of Guilin entices one to enter, to be embraced by it.

In Oriental landscape painting there is usually a small figure, a little boat, a hut that leads the viewer into the miniature landscape. When I was walking in the hills of Guilin, I felt I had wandered into a Chinese painting. This intimate feeling that Guilin especially gives has produced a wealth of Chinese paintings and poetry all through the centuries. It inspired the appreciation of nature that became the very essence of Taoist thinking. Lao Zi, China's great philosopher, wrote that the ideal Taoist is a person who avoids conventional social obligations and leads a simple, spontaneous and meditative life close to nature. I believe that in Guilin one can fully experience this "closeness to nature."

I went to Guilin over ten years ago, before it was officially opened to tourism. I was moved and was reminded of the many poems I had read about its beauty: Fan Chengda of the Song Dynasty wrote: "Guilin is the only place where you can with one sweep of the eyes, see numberless peaks springing from flat ground like jade bamboo shoots, jostling one another." When I stood on top of the Lonely Eminence Hill, that rises abruptly five hundred feet from ground level, I thought of a poem that Zhang Gu wrote in the Tang Dynasty:

> The Lonely Eminence Hill stands aloof.
> Its peak points towards the clouds straining to reach them.
> It bridges the gap between heaven and earth.
> This sky-supporting pillar of the south.

In the Qing Dynasty, Yuan Mei had another interpretation of the Lonely Eminence Hill:

> No traces of its origin, no clues of parentage,
> Dropped from the sky, a lonely peak!
> Strange are the hills of Guilin, nine out of ten,
> But the Lonely Eminence is the strangest of them all!
> Three hundred and sixty steps lead to the summit,
> And when you get there lo! the whole city is under your feet!
> If a hill can be as straight as a stretched string,
> For a man, what's wrong in being upright and aloof?

The weather of Guilin is capricious. "When it rains, it is cold; when the sun shines, it is hot; be it spring or summer, autumn or winter." The many caves of Guilin are quite cool. Luti, or Reed Pipe Cave, three miles from the center of Guilin on the Peach Blossom River, Tao Hua Jiang, is renowned for its fairyland interior. With an entrance well hidden by tall grass and boulders, it was long forgotten though, as early as the tenth century, during the Song Dynasty, the cave served as a refuge for political fugitives. It was only rediscovered in 1959.

The beauty of Guilin is only surpassed by that of nearby Yangshuo. I sailed down the River Li in October. That shallow river had just enough water to let us navigate, water so clear that I could see the pebbles on the bottom. Every bend during that six hour trip was full of surprises and exquisite scenery: hills reflected in perfect symmetry, a fisherman alone on a bamboo raft with his cormorant—a bird trained to catch fish. On the shore, I saw a hundred-year-old banyan tree. I was fortunate to sail in a boat without a motor, punted all the way.

Eighty miles downriver was Picture Hill, Hua Shan, so called because with much imagination one may see nine horses on the uneven surface of the slopes. Ancient scholars on their way to the imperial examination in the capital believed that if they saw all nine horses they would win a first place in the exam. The more they could see, the higher the place. I was ready to believe this too when before my eyes reality was so unreal. The Song Dynasty poet, Zhou Hao, attributed Guilin's extraordinary beauty to divine doing:

> How many thousand years ago was this screen carved?
> The more it has been beaten by rain and wind, the clearer the images
> They were painted by a drunken god, I believe.
> See with what supernatural power the strokes were done.

Midway between Guilin and Yangshuo, Xing Ping was the climax of my trip.

> Peaks and crags hang upside down and hills float on the water.
> Scenery, so beautiful, unrivaled by a painting.

Ji Bei wrote what is my favorite poem on Guilin.

> There is a man reflected on the water;
> And on the water there is a floating moon,
> When the water flows, the moon does stay,
> When the moon is gone, the water flows on.

Along with Li Bo's similar thought:

> The moon is bright and the autumn waters cold:
> The water flows on but the moon stays.
> I love to look at both, trimming my white hair.

Guilin was one of the first places I visited in China. I came to it with the poetry I had learned as a child still ringing in my ears, even after the years spent as a student in Europe and America. Nowadays, with many more people visiting Guilin, it is not quite as easy to imitate the experience of the ancient poets or to sleep in a small boat as I was able to, "waking up to the sound of sculling," as Han Yu said in one poem. I think it was in Guilin that I first learned to enter into the landscape, rather than trying to understand or to conquer it. I learned to find my own place in nature. And it was this trip to Guilin that prompted me to spend the next ten years coming back again and again to China in search of quiet beauty.

桂林山勢天下雄　陽朔一竟多奇峯

漁舟逐水愛山春

72

突然一峯插南斗

夕陽無限好　只是近黃昏

SOUTH
OF
THE
YANGZI

SOUTH OF THE YANGZI
Suzhou: Marco Polo's "Venice of the East," and Tong Li

I wanted to see Suzhou because of an old Chinese saying of the Song Dynasty: "We have heaven above, Suzhou and Hangzhou below."

The walled city of Suzhou dates back to 514 B.C. It attained importance when Prince He Lu of the State of Wu made it his capital and enlarged it from one kilometer and a half to twenty three kilometers in circumference. Seven hundred years ago, Marco Polo said in his "Travels": "Suzhou is a very great and noble city. The people possess silk in great quantities, from which they make gold brocade and other stuffs, and they live by their manufacture and trade."

Gusu (another name for Suzhou) is the setting of the "Mooring at Night by the Maple Bridge," a poem by Zhang Ji of the Tang Dynasty. This is one of the poems I learned as a child and it is familiar to most Chinese school children anywhere:

> The moon sets, a lone crow caws across the frosty sky
> As the fishing boat's lights flicker sadly under the Maple Bridge.
> Beyond the city the bell of Cold Hill Temple chimes
> For the coming of a guest boat in the night.

The scenery, a mild climate, prosperity and the cultural heritage from the north, all helped to build Suzhou into a "garden city." The Grand Canal with a total length of one thousand seven hundred and ninety-four kilometers (one thousand one hundred and twenty-one miles) is one of the longest man-made waterways in the world. With its terminals at Beijing and at Hangzhou (not far from Suzhou), this was an important navigation channel linking China's north and south. Like the Great Wall, it shows tremendous engineering skills for its time. The first digging began in 496 B.C. in western Suzhou as a military measure during the reign of King Fu Chai of the State of Wu, and was continued section by section in succeeding dynasties. Most of it was built by the Emperor

Yang Di of the Sui Dynasty for his pleasure trips down to Yangzhou where he liked to enjoy the "qiong" blossoms, a flower—now extinct—of apparently great beauty and fragrance.

In Suzhou, I saw the Cold Hill Temple (Han Shan Si) that Zhang Ji described in his poem as well as the Maple Bridge across the Grand Canal. A city map dating back to the Song Dynasty, carved in stone, is preserved in the Suzhou Museum and shows the area criss-crossed by six north-south and fourteen east-west canals spanned by more than three hundred and fifty bridges. The streets run parallel to the canals lined with houses. From their back doors, steps lead down to the water. Today, just as in the Song Dynasty, people do their washing in the canals or draw water from them.

Another poet of the Tang Dynasty wrote:

> Have you ever been in Suzhou
> Where every house pillows on water?
> Ancient palaces filled with pavilions.
> Canals and bridges too many to count.
> Buy caltrops and lotus root at a night market;
> Silks and satins weigh down junks in the spring...

The people of Suzhou are justly proud of its gardens. In limited space, they present an endless variety of views and effects. By cleverly "borrowing" from the surrounding scenery, they create an impression of space. They stimulate the visitor's imagination. Tablets inscribed with poems placed strategically here and there add to the poetic atmosphere. To me, the most picturesque are the "water streets" with their old bridges, people going about their business in their rowboats as they have always done.

A friend, Cheng Duoduo, a Chinese painter from Shanghai, once told me of a lovely little village, Tong Li, still true to its traditional ways. Only twenty kilometers from Suzhou, but surrounded by five lakes, it was formerly accessible only by water. Recently, a road was built and its inhabitants can now go off to Suzhou by bus. To reach Tong Li, which is not marked except on the most detailed maps of the area, I had first to travel to Suzhou. I flew from Hong Kong to Shanghai, then took a train for a one and a half hour trip. The scenery was of little interest: industrial areas interspersed with some cultivated land. The sight of the Tiger Hill Pagoda (Hu Qiu) that dates back to the Spring and Autumn period announced that we were arriving in Suzhou. As the city has not expanded much beyond its original layout, the narrow streets are congested with buses and bicycles. It was early April, the maples that line the sidewalks were still bare, revealing the gray slanted tile roofs. I dropped my bags at the Suzhou Hotel. After another two-hour drive, by car this time, I was greeted at Tong Li by a helpful local official, Mr. Jiang, who guided me around his maze-like village. In the pouring rain, I experienced a little of the ancient tranquillity of this place. In its thousand year history, it has produced many scholars, poets and painters. One garden dates to the Qing Dynasty. It first belonged to a retired government official, who, weary of court intrigue, built it for himself. He called it "The Garden of Retreat to Contemplate": Tuisiyuan. These three characters are brush painted on the black wall above its modest entrance. Within is a miniature replica of its surroundings: pavilions built beside tiny canals. Unlike the well-known and often crowded gardens of Suzhou, one can savour in peace the tranquil elegance of this once private park.

Mr. Jiang was both surprised and delighted by my interest in little known Tong Li. We sipped tea in one of the pavilions listening to the rain. He told me that thirty percent of the houses in Tong Li date from the Ming and the early Qing dynasties. In a very small area with ten thousand inhabitants are forty nine bridges. He told me that I had come just a little early in the season: in a few weeks, with spring in full bloom, the local residents would set out ten thousand pots of bougainvillea on their porches. The maples lining the canals would be green, casting shade over the waterways. We walked in the rain over many bridges: one more than eight hundred years old, others built at least in the Qing Dynasty. Pu An Bridge was originally built in 1506 and later restored. Mr. Jiang explained that from the different colors of slabs in the bridge one can deduce the period that the repairs were made. As in Venice, many of Tong Li's houses rise straight from the water. Peculiar to this village, people have used hollow wine flasks as part of the walls thinking a thief would make noise clambering over these pieces. How effective this can be against burglars I do not know; however, I did find the result decorative and colorful.

The rain had almost stopped; school children were carrying their umbrellas on their way home. An old woman sitting outside her simple house, her face too wrinkled to get any older, smiled at me. She still had bound feet: I guess she was born at the end of the last century.

The next day, I visited another "water village," Lu Ze. Already more influenced by modern ways, there are the inevitable television antennas on the roofs of many ancient houses. I returned to wander around Tong Li alone. I lost myself in its maze, far back in history.

Before leaving the area, I went to the better known gardens of Suzhou. They have interesting names, like Humble Administrator's Garden, Lingering Garden, Garden of Ease... When they were built, I am sure they were miniature worlds in which retired civil servants or wealthy merchants lived out lives of intrigue among their concubines. Nowadays, they have become havens for Chinese on their outings as well as tourists from the four corners of the world. I am afraid I don't have enough imagination to feel the elegant atmosphere that once prevailed. But in Tong Li, inside the "Garden of Retreat to Contemplate" I found what I was looking for in my search for the quiet beauty of China.

畫船聽雨眠

君到姑蘇見　人家盡枕河

QUIET TIME
QUIET PLACES

QUIET TIME, QUIET PLACES

For the first-time visitor, the immediate impression of China is of crowds. The streets of Beijing, Shanghai, Xi'an and Guangzhou are packed with people. The stores are filled with shoppers and browsers, the parks with passersby. China's quiet beauty is not obvious. In a country where the population is unevenly distributed, over two-thirds of the territory is made up of uncultivated mountain, hill and desert country. There is much natural beauty in these. Less obvious is the quiet beauty found at quiet times and in quiet places in the crowded areas.

From the Sino-Nepalese border at the west, from the high mountain range that includes Mount Everest, two great rivers flow eastward through China towards the Pacific: the Changjiang, better known as the Yangzi and the Huanghe or Yellow River. Most of the one billion Chinese are concentrated in the parts of China through which these rivers flow and along some coastal areas. The soil is fertile, the land relatively flat. Sichuan, bisected by the Changjiang, is known as a land of abundance. Another area, the Yangzi Delta, is called "Land of Fish and Rice," broad and smooth, rising no more than ten meters (thirty-three feet) above sea level, woven with secondary rivers and streams.

Apart from those areas already crowded with their own inhabitants, the foreign visitor must cope with China's phenomenal domestic tourism. A billion people travel within China itself to the famous destinations, parks and gardens, on honeymoons or vacations, pausing before the monuments or the most scenic spots to take photographs of themselves as a record of their travels.

At the end of my boat trip down the Yangzi Gorges, I visited the Yueyang Gardens in Hunan Province on the day before the park was officially reopened after a year of renovation. I had the good fortune to savor quietly the beauty of the pavilions overlooking the Dongting Lake, originally built by the governor of Yueyang during the Tang Dynasty, then rebuilt under the supervision of poet Fan Zhongyan, when he was in exile under the Song Dynasty. Sitting there by myself, I thought of his writing, of the passage where he says: "In the Dongting Lake, where one can see the endless faraway mountains and the rushing water, where the beauty of nature changes from morning to evening, where one can see the numerous changes of nature herself, lies the pavilion of Yueyang..." In the Tang Dynasty, another well-known poet, Meng Haoran described the pavilion in August when the water was calm and the air cool. Feeling sad in the city of Yueyang with no boat to take him away, he sat quietly watching a patient fisherman plying his trade. To him, it was a wondrous sight and he felt a stab of envy. A thousand years later, I could watch a similar sight. But the next day, after the pavilion was opened to the public, people arrived from all over China; the entire garden exploded with them; some even climbed up the trees to avoid the stampede. Needless to say, my poetic quiet beauty had evaporated.

Of course, at the most scenic spots that are now well-known, it is not always possible to beat the crowds for a whole day. Some I was lucky to visit before too many Chinese and foreign tourists arrived. Often, it is a matter of timing during the day and even more of being ready with one's eye and one's camera to perceive the quiet beauty at unexpected times and unexpected places.

Huangshan and Emeishan were once mainly pilgrim destinations, besides serving as inspiration for the occasional poet and painter who wandered for days to absorb the essence of the landscape. For my early photographs of these areas, I found them relatively uncrowded. Later, I was sometimes able to return to photograph the same place at less popular hours of the day.

I remember seeing "Lonely Eminence Hill" in Guilin at dawn, then again at sunset and by moonlight; each time it projected a different mood. Low wooden houses stretched as far as the eye could see. From among them abruptly rose the elegant small hill, rising a hundred and fifty meters above the center of the town. The search for harmonious beauty sometimes conflicts with development and progress. The delicate balance of the little wooden houses against the hill could so easily be destroyed by concrete high rises built with the worthy intention of accommodating all the tourists who would like to see its beauty. This is another reason why it is desirable to arrive somewhat ahead of the others. To me, it is well worth enduring the lack of facilities in an area before its touristic development in exchange for the opportunity of quiet contemplation.

But I alone am responsible for being ready to see the beauty that is there: although there is no such thing as getting a good photograph by sheer luck, some of my favorite photographs were taken as by chance. When traveling through towns, villages or cities, as much as in the scenic areas, I am always ready to focus on the beautiful or the unusual.

I remember, for instance, the time when I was returning from Yangshuo to Guilin by road. I saw a mother carrying her baby. She held an orange parasol against the backdrop of almost translucent hills. The orange dot of color brought the focal point to the landscape, accenting the blue green fields: a typical Chinese painting presented itself for an instant only with this little human figure exactly in the right place. Another time, on a visit to the Great Wall in midwinter when most tourists are deterred by the severe cold, I saw some people pushing their bicycles uphill. In the distance was the silhouette of the Great Wall, the battlements hazily offset against the pale winter sky. Pointing my camera slightly into the sun, I obtained a monochromatic effect, emphasizing the slant of a single tree that balanced the composition.

The Temple of Heaven in Beijing gets crowded when the first tour buses arrive in the morning. I like to go as do the natives, at sunrise. People, mostly elderly, can be seen shadowboxing under a graceful pine. One old man was doing his leg exercises while reading the morning paper.

Elsewhere, among the hurried crowds of visitors, the great calm and beauty of a Buddha may be overlooked. For instance, a ferry boat regularly rushes the tourists past the colossal Buddha of Leshan in Sichuan. Because of the rapid current of the River Minjiang, they have barely enough time to take a quick snapshot. I negotiated a rowboat from a local fishing family and moored by a sandy island in the middle of the river directly across from the statue: I waited until the afternoon sun lit up the Buddha's peaceful, serene face.

The Chinese come and look for the renowned beauty of Guilin, of Huangshan, and begin to come to recently discovered Juizhaigou for its natural beauty. At least, it has already attracted some hardy visitors, especially painters.

There are also vignettes of ordinary Chinese life that hold great charm for me but that most Chinese visitors pass by as banal. In Xi'an, I looked into a courtyard: the position of the two bare trees in winter and the accent colors of the hanging laundry placed exactly in the square format of a photograph evoked a great sense of design. In its simplicity, I found something typical of many homes in China. Such commonplace charm may seem more interesting and striking to someone who lives mostly in large, western cities. On my trip down the gorges of the Yangzi, it was an abandoned whitewashed house against the rolling hills that suddenly touched me, its loneliness humble against the grandeur of the hillside.

I was drawn to many places because I had read about them as a child, in poems and old travel writings. I was not always able to recapture the quiet beauty that my ancient sources had made me expect; but, by choosing either a quiet place or a quiet time ahead of others or in the off season and through a feeling of great expectation that kept me ready for the inner calm I was seeking, I did find it time and again, with a quiet eye and a quiet mind.

古佛臨流都坐斷

幽僻囂塵外

TIBET:
LHASA
AND
SHIGATSE

Looking at a map of Asia, I often wondered what life was like in faraway Tibet, isolated from the rest of the world by high mountain ranges, remote and mysterious. One day I came across a painting done by a court painter for the Emperor Tai Zong in the Tang Dynasty. It showed the marriage of Princess Wen Cheng to the Tibetan King Songzan Ganbu in the seventh century. I found records of this event, embellished no doubt by legend, that told how this young Tibetan King, at the age of sixteen, dreamt that he was to ask in marriage the princesses of Nepal and of China, both of whom born with divine inspiration,and that both would bring with them images of Buddha. He immediately sent out a minister as an envoy to make his dream come true. The mission succeeded in Nepal and brought Princess Bhrikuti Devi to Tibet but failed time and again to obtain the consent of the Emperor of China. The beauty and intelligence of the Chinese princess were legendary and emissaries of suitors from as far away as India were stationed in Changan (present-day Xi'an) to ask for her hand. The fifth time the Tibetan minister arrived with five thousand taels of gold, with silver, pearls, elephants and horses. The Emperor was touched by his sincerity as well as impressed by the capability of Songzan Ganbu who had reigned since he was thirteen and had become the first king to unify all Tibet under one rule. Thus, as recorded in painting and folklore, the Princess departed for faraway Tibet with an entourage of musicians, craftsmen and builders, bringing classic Chinese poetry, religious rites, medical books "with four hundred and four cures," medical instruments and an abundance of precious stones. True to the prophecy, she also brought with her a bejewelled image of Gautama Buddha, as the crowned Bodhisattva. Princess Wen Cheng was received with great jubilation and her knowledge touched off admiration for the more advanced culture of China, initiating a tradition of scholars journeying from Tibet to study in China. The King was converted to Buddhism by his two consorts. And Buddhism, with its rich and refined traditions of architecture, sculpture, painting, its music and liturgy, its sacred scriptures made a great contribution to Tibetan civilization. To this day, Tibetans remain devout Buddhists.

Princess Wen Cheng must have truly fallen in love with the people of Tibet, because after the death of Songzan Ganbu at the age of thirty-four, she spent the remaining forty years of her life in her adopted country. She was buried there and the Tibetans erected temples in her memory.

My own trip to Tibet, thirteen centuries later, was to me no less exotic than it must have been to Princess Wen Cheng. I started my journey from Hong Kong, transiting overnight in Guangzhou to reach Chengdu in Sichuan, the gateway to western China. Tibet, until recently, was isolated from the rest of the world, practically inaccessible until the construction of the Sichuan-Tibet road, some twelve hundred and fifty tortuous miles that cross over a dozen high mountain ranges. I had the choice of going to Tibet by this road, which would have taken half a month from Sichuan or of flying for three hours. Although I was warned that the sudden change from the lowlands to Lhasa's three thousand six hundred and forty meters (some twelve thousand feet) could cause high-altitude sickness, I preferred to spend more time in Tibet than getting there. The view from the plane was spectacular: an immense plateau surrounded by the world's highest mountains. The Tibetans have a poem dating from the sixth century that closely describes my initial impression of Tibet:

> This center of heaven
> This core of earth
> This heart of the world
> Fenced round with snow.

August is the best month to visit Tibet: the days are warm, the mornings and nights are comfortable, at least with a sweater; a little like summer weather in Los Angeles. I chose to go alone to Lhasa in August 1985, knowing that if I should suffer from severe altitude sickness, I would be able to change my plans and leave at any time without ruining the pleasure of others. Because they are scarce in Lhasa, I had also been advised to bring fresh fruit and vegetables from Chengdu.

The towns in Tibet usually have a few thousand inhabitants, centered around a Buddhist monastery. The only real city is Lhasa, the capital, with sixty thousand inhabitants. Shigatse is the next most important town. Most of my time in Tibet was spent in exploring these two places.

On arrival in Lhasa, the high-altitude sickness crept up on me gradually.

I landed at noon, feeling fine, and enjoyed the hundred mile drive, partly along a river, that took over three hours from the airport to Lhasa. What struck me most was the barren landscape. My driver told me the road had recently been paved. It used to take him twice as long on the former rocky road. My room, an ordinary looking bungalow with simple facilities seemed to me more in keeping with the surroundings than the comfort of the big modern hotel soon to be opened in the new part of Lhasa.

By evening, I could no longer stand up. I was told that I was drained of color, a typical case of high-altitude sickness. A doctor was at hand to give me medicine and a portable oxygen supply which looked like a hot water-bottle with a rubber tube. Primitive yet effective: I only needed to tie a knot in the tube when I finished inhaling from it.

My first sight of the Potala in the evening glow at moonrise made me fully aware of the magic of Tibet. Was this the sort of vision that retained the Chinese Princess here? Among the magnificent murals at the Potala, I was most interested in the scene showing the minister as an envoy at the Chinese court asking for the hand of Princess Wen Cheng on behalf of the Tibetan King. Another, of the joyous reception of Princess Wen Cheng in Tibet echoes the oft-told tale.

> When the Princess consents to come to Tibet,
> No one is afraid of the vast sandbars
> And there are a hundred steeds to meet you.
> No one is afraid of the snow-capped mountains,
> And there are a hundred dzos to greet you.
> No one is afraid of the surging rivers,
> And there are a hundred cowhide boats to welcome you.

The murals of the Potala were begun in 1648. Sixty-six of the finest Tibetan artists of the time worked on them for over a decade. Among the treasures inside the palace is a copy of the Mahaprajnaparamita Sutra written in gold letters and Buddhist scriptures written on patra, palm leaves from ancient India. To the Buddhists, the Potala houses not only their history but is also the dwelling of divine power. In the dimly lit rooms, many of which never admit daylight, are seated lamas, chanting the Buddhist canon by the light of butter lamps. Devotees, many of whom arrive from afar, prayer wheel in one hand, prayer beads in the other, move silently observing the old rule of walking along the very edge of the stairs. The Potala wears a thousand faces, and at different times, from different vantage points, I marveled at its infinite variety.

I was told that Songzan Ganbu chose Rasa, "the Goat Land," for his residence. Later it became known as Lhasa, "the God's Land." On a steep hill north of the plains, he built a large palace said to resemble a sleeping elephant and called it the "White Royal Residence." The King enlarged it for his two Princesses from afar. Eventually, it rose nine stories high with nine hundred rooms but then fell into decay. The "Potala" today, is largely a new structure started in 1642, a thousand years later, on the same site. The influence of Chinese "golden" roofs with stacked eaves and the Indian wooden structure blended together harmoniously to become the unique Tibetan style of architecture.

From the Jokhang Temple, one has a panoramic view of the brick walls of the Potala Palace, originally built by Songzan Ganbu to welcome his Nepalese Princess. The front gate faces her native land. The golden roofs gleam blindingly in the noon sun, their ridges decorated with urns, pearls, golden bells and animals of cast metal. Dragons and hanging bells at the tips of the soaring eaves lend a touch from the Chinese monasteries to the building. Within is the most sacred Buddhist image, the statue brought to Tibet by the Chinese Princess. Among other works of art is also a statue of Songzan Ganbu flanked by his two foreign Princesses.

Long lines of pilgrims form at dawn outside the Jokhang temple to wait for their turn to light the butter lamps inside. Many had come from afar, sometimes journeying for months, the pads under their elbows and knees well-worn from often prostrating themselves along the way. My camera flash, so embarrassingly out of place, was largely ignored.

A short car ride from the Jokhang temple is the Drepung monastery, built in 1416. It is one of Lhasa's great monasteries. Imposing in architecture, sprawling at the foot of a hill, it consists of a number of buildings at various levels conforming to the terrain. All is orderly, symmetrical and stately, yet not rigid. Inside it is built like a town. I photographed lamas threading their way through the alleyways. Preserved in the Drepung Monastery, among other art treasures is the magnificent statue of Buddha Champa.

Every day in Tibet, I was becoming more acclimatized to the altitude. With a driver and a guide, I went to Shigatse, wearing a wide-brimmed hat to protect my face from the extremely strong ultraviolet rays. I was much distressed by the way my chain smoking companions burned up the valuable oxygen in the car. For relief, I inhaled from my rubber bag, especially after stops when I had exhausted myself running around to take photographs. We drove three hundred and sixty-seven kilometers in ten hours, part of the way along Lake Yamdrok, one of the large freshwater lakes in Tibet. My driver stopped by the shore and we were able to catch an abundance of fish with our bare hands. They made a delicious meal that evening. Later I found out that while the Tibetans practice celestial burial for most of the dead, the corpses of beggars and the very poor are thrown into the water. In the water burial, the feeding of a corpse to the fish has the spiritual significance of a gift to Buddha and so fulfills the wish to perform good work. In former times, fish were considered "gods of the river," and to eat them was contrary to the Buddhist faith.

The profound impact of Buddhism on the people of Tibet was in evidence all along the remote road far from any town. There, I saw pilgrims prostrating themselves at regular intervals as they went along. On the peak of many mountains, the Tibetans place small cairns of stones and something rather like a flag to signal the holiness of the spot. The road went as high as four thousand nine hundred and ninety-five meters, a vantage point from which we could see several glaciers.

On the way back to Lhasa, we made a few unexpected stops: my driver felt it his duty to repair a broken down vehicle as self-reliance and helping one another is the code of the road. Traffic on the highway was scarce. We encountered three Tibetans on donkeys, then a few yaks, valued as much for carrying loads as for their meat. Later, we saw a young man hauling on his own back a boat made from cowhide.

In Shigatse, I decided against photographing the celestial burial where the corpse is torn limb from limb until every piece of the human flesh has been fed to the vultures. To me, death, as much as birth is sacred and therefore ultimately private.

I visited another splendid monastery, the Trashilungpo, founded in 1447. Inside, was a stupendous and colossal statue of Buddha Maitreya, standing over eighty-seven feet tall, gilded with more than ten thousand ounces of gold.

Superb frescoes, exquisite engravings on the bronze door-knockers of the gates of the Potala, Buddhist statues of metal, clay, stone and carved wood, images painted on satin and cloth adorn the interior of the Palace, temples and monasteries. I believe that such beauty can only have come from divine inspiration. An inspiration that, I hope, is still present and will protect this ancient culture. The people of Tibet, living on their high plateaus, face not only the harsh wind, snow and severe cold but also the winds of change. Now, no longer isolated, they have to adapt to modern life while preserving their traditions and Buddhist beliefs.

In the jet age, no place is remote not even faraway Tibet. My visit allowed me a brief glimpse, unlike Princess Wen Cheng who once she had left China never did return. That took great courage. As did, as recently as 1923, the trip of Alexandra David-Neel. "I craved to go beyond the garden gate, to follow the road that passed it by, and to set out for the unknown," she wrote, becoming the first white woman to enter, at fifty-five, the then-forbidden Tibetan capital. She ended her account of that trip: "The first white woman had entered forbidden Lhasa and shown the way. May others follow and open with loving heart the gates of the wonderland 'for the good, for the welfare of many' as the Buddhist scriptures say." Let us hope today's travelers to this magic city in the Himalayas come to look at it "for the good, for the welfare of many" indeed and leave it undisturbed.

深宮高樓入紫清

CONCLUSION AND ACKNOWLEDGMENTS

My early photographs may have crystallized a short time in China's long history. My book, "Faces of China," published in 1973, was but a brief impression. "Quiet Beauty of China" is the result of many trips spanning a decade. This project of photographing China was to be a personal journey of discovery. Li Bo traveled with his wine flask. With my Hasselblad and all its attachments, my steps are not as light. After sunset in the quietness of wherever I find myself, I jot down notes. I talk to people, collect anecdotes. I rarely return to the same place: there is yet another mountain to climb.

In many traditional Chinese paintings, a man walks alone in nature with little encumbrance. For thousands of years, along the trodden paths, travellers left behind them no more than their footprints. It is not always so today. My adventure in China in search of beauty first began in solitude; more recently, I took my little son, Lingshan, "Enchanted Mountain." We climbed Mount Emei, sailed down the Yangzi River and explored Jiuzhaigou together. I cannot be certain that when he is grown up the footsteps of Li Bo will not be covered with paper and styrofoam.

My adult life has been a search for harmony. I was born in a noisy, teeming city where I spent my childhood with few trees, just the bustling waterfront: Hong Kong. In China, I can still find harmony through its quiet beauty—timeless... as long as time allows.

The painters and poets of ancient China showed us the wealth of beauty that they found in their world. As a child in Hong Kong, I memorized the Tang dynasty poems, often without knowing their meaning. The world of Li Bo, Wang Wei—of lofty mountains, meandering rivers, thundering waterfalls and whimsical clouds made up the early part of my image of China. I was in search of this world.

Included in this book are my favorite places, the setting of my dream world: one mountain, Huangshan; one river, the Lijiang; a primeval forest, Jiuzhaigou; a faraway plateau, Lhasa; and a small village, Tong Li. A few photographs grouped under the title

"Quiet Time, Quiet Places" were taken outside Beijing, near Chengdu and somewhere along the banks of the Yangzi River near Chongqing. The precise location is of no particular importance; they are vignettes of the beauty in ordinary life, perhaps too common to be noticed.

The photographs in this book were taken during the past ten years—the earlier ones of Guilin before the influx of tourists, of Huangshan before the cable cars, of Jiuzhaigou before its development into a national park and of Lhasa before the opening of high rise hotels.

Opening up such sites as tourist destinations inevitably entails compromise, but also renews interest in China's cultural heritage: even little villages like Tong Li are being preserved, along with other historical and scenic places. I trust in the endurance of their remarkable beauty as a continuing inspiration for more poems and paintings. My photographs are but a few images of personal interpretation, to share my own quiet moments in the beauty of China.

I chose photography as my medium of interpreting the traditional subjects. I consider photography a visual language, a language without words that enables me to communicate to all. It takes only a split second to record an event. I like to practice the art of choosing from a host of events what is interesting and important, working in the dark room cropping and eliminating the irrelevant or enhancing a particular mood.

I like the honesty of photographing people and things exactly as I find them, without posing, rearranging or disturbing them, in order to produce a spontaneous record of a particular moment in time. I do go back time and again to find the right lighting to interpret the subject. The time of the year is of particular importance. Guilin and Jiuzhaigou are at their best in October, Tibet in August, Huangshan in May and Tong Li in the spring. Before going, I did very little research about the places I went to photograph. I wanted to react to them as intuitively as possible.

In writing about "Quiet Beauty of China," I referred to the notes I had taken during my trips, consulted books and scholars. I have quoted translations of poems from T. C. Lai's "Kweilin, China's Most Scenic Spot." Alan Nichols, who shares my love for nature in China, contributed the charming story about Pei Du. My list of thanks could go on and on: to the many friendly hands who helped me with my travels in China, to the people in official capacities who facilitated my trips and introduced me to places.

I am particularly grateful to Professor Jao Tsung-I, an internationally known Chinese poet, calligrapher and painter, embodying the "three perfections" of a traditional Chinese scholar and artist. When I consulted him in Hong Kong, he kindly read the text and wrote the calligraphy for this book.

Each meeting with Julien van der Wal, an accomplished graphic artist who designed the book, and his wife Jacqueline was an inspiration. Their studio outside Geneva, a converted farmhouse, exudes harmony and tranquillity, a perfect place for the birth of "Quiet Beauty of China."

I owe much to my husband, John van Praag, a scholar of ancient Greek and Latin, whose own deep and passionate interest in the classics enables him to appreciate my efforts and research. My thanks go to him for reviewing and editing my text.

My little son, Lingshan, accompanied me to Jiuzhaigou and climbed with me to the top of Mount Emei. Through his innocent eyes, I was made aware of some aspects of beauty that I might have missed. My desire to preserve a little of my world for him inspired me to put together "Quiet Beauty of China."

Pat Fok
August 1987

B.C. 722-481	Spring and Autumn Period
c. 6th C	Lao Zi, Taoist philosopher
514-496	Prince He Lu, King of Wu
c. 500	Building of Suzhou begun by Wu Zixu
c. 496	Beginning of the Grand Canal in Western Suzhou
c. 400	First walls for defense built by the Warring States
214	Walls of the Qin, Zhao and Yan linked together into the "Great Wall"
A.D. 65	Introduction of Buddhism in China
222-280	State of Wu
581-618	Sui Dynasty
604-617	Emperor Yan Di
early 7th C	Further construction of the Grand Canal
7th C	Initial construction of the Potala Palace
618-649	King Songzan Ganbu of Tibet
618-907	Tang Dynasty
627-649	Tang Emperor Tai Zong; the peak of ancient Chinese culture
689-740	Meng Haoran, poet
701-761	Wang Wei, poet
701-762	Li Bo, poet
712-770	Du Fu, poet
713	Building of Great Buddha of Leshan begun
715-780	Zhang Ji, poet
768-824	Han Yu, poet
772-846	Bai Juji, poet
813-858	Li Shangyin, poet
846-904	Du Xunhe, poet
9th C	Zhang Gu, poet

960-1279	Song Dynasty
989-1052	Fan Zhongyan, poet
1060-1111	Zhou Hao, poet
1126-1193	Fan Chengda, poet
1271-1368	Yuan Dynasty, rule of the Mongols
1274-1291	Marco Polo in Dadu (Beijing)
1368-1644	Ming Dynasty
1403-1424	The Great Wall extended and rebuilt
1416	Building of the Drepung Monastery in Lhasa
1447	The construction of Trashilungpo Monastery in Tibet
1586-1641	Xu Xiake, travel writer
1610-1664	Hong Ren, painter
1623-1697	Mei Qing, painter
1641-1708	Shi Tao, painter
1642	Rebuilding of the Potala Palace in Lhasa
n.d.	Zhang Fengyu, poet
1644-1911	Qing Dynasty
1716-1797	Yuan Mei, poet
n.d.	Xu Jinghi, minor poet of Qing Dynasty

HUANGSHAN

19 They were painted by a drunken god, I believe.
 See with what supernatural power the strokes were done.
 Zhou Hao, Song Dynasty
21 Ten thousand trees hidden deep in clouds.
 Du Fu, Tang Dynasty
25 In the jade green sky clouds reside
 Bai Juji, Tang Dynasty
26 Surely these clouds must join the sea
 This mighty ocean cannot be clouds
27 I wish I could sail on the wind in a skiff
 To see the Lord of Emptiness on the Three Peaks.
 Xu Jinghi, Qing Dynasty
28 Is it a painting, I wonder, or a dream.
 Zhang Fengyu, Ming Dynasty
32 How clear are the mountains after the new rain.
 Wang Wei, Tang Dynasty

JIUZHAIGOU

44 At the summit temple:
 Raise my hand, touch the stars,
45 Whispering for fear of wakening those in Heaven.
 Li Bo, Tang Dynasty
46 This river so clear that it cleanses my heart.
 Li Bo, Tang Dynasty
49 Like the peach blossoms in yonder brook
 I flow away calmly...
 'Tis another sky and earth, not the world of man.
 Li Bo, Tang Dynasty
51 Like the Milky Way pouring down from Heaven.
 Li Bo, Tang Dynasty
53 The water of the lake is clear and the wind of the forest is pure.
 Du Fu, Tang Dynasty
55 Autumn water clear, its depth unfathomed.
 Du Fu, Tang Dynasty

GUILIN

65 Extraordinary are the mountain ranges of Guilin
 But under the sun most extraordinary of all is Yangshuo.
 Zhang Luanguei, Qing Dynasty
70 A fisherman drifts with the current, entranced by the spring hills.
 Wang Wei, Tang Dynasty
74 Dropped from the sky, a lonely peak!
 Yuan Mei, Qing Dynasty
76 Softly the sun sets on the day too brief.
 Li Shangyin, Tang Dynasty.

SUZHOU

86 To fall asleep in the painted barge,
 Listening to the rain.
 Wei Zhuang, Tang Dynasty
89 Have you ever been in Suzhou
 Where every house pillows on water?
 Tu Xuanhe, Tang Dynasty

QUIET TIME, QUIET PLACES

102 The ancient Buddha on the river's edge still sits...
 Fan Chengda, Tang Dynasty
106 Living quietly far from the noise and dust of man.
 Bai Juji, Tang Dynasty

TIBET

123 In this Palace, whose pavilions pierce the sky.
 Li Bo, Tang Dynasty

宇宙九月吉
法京陶毫
齊白